MW00633849

Marblehead

Light

Marblehead Light

Latitude   42° 30′ 20″ N

Longitude   70° 50′ 03″ W

All proceeds from the sale of this book go to the
Town of Marblehead Historical Commission
Abbot Hall, 188 Washington Street, Marblehead, MA 01945
www.marbleheadhistory.org

Page 1: The yacht *Harpoon* sailing off Marblehead Neck, c. 1892. The original lighthouse with its temporary 100-foot mast is clearly visible in the background.

Page 3: Ladies and a gentleman pose at Crocker Park, overlooking Marblehead Harbor with the iconic Light tower visible in the distance on the Neck, 1898.

Marblehead

The Story of a New England Icon

Light

by Bill Conly

Town of Marblehead Historical Commission

Marblehead Light:
The Story of a New England Icon
by Bill Conly

Editor: Frances B. King, HistoryKeep.com

Published by the Town of Marblehead Historical Commission © 2017

Abbot Hall, 188 Washington Street, Marblehead, MA 01945

www.marbleheadhistory.org

Printed in Canada

ISBN: 978-0-9989879-0-3

Book and cover design: Amy Drinker, Aster Designs

This book was set in 10.5-point ITC Giovanni with Poppl-Laudatio display type.

The paper stock is 100 LB Sterling Premium Matte.

First Edition

10 9 8 7 6 5 4 3 2 1

To the generations of fishermen, sailors, and ferryboat captains

who have passed this point of land since the 1600s:

may the Light be a guide into the future.

One-design yachts sail past Marblehead Light, c. 1910

We have a good harbour and wish to make it easy access to the care worn

and weather beaten mariner, so that he may find easily

a haven of safety if not the haven of his desires.

Marblehead Town Meeting Minutes, c. 1832

Marblehead Harbor, with the causeway (right) to the Neck,
and Marblehead Light at the tip (left) of the Neck, c. 2011

Table of Contents

TOP: Bathers in the cove at the edge of the Marblehead lighthouse property, c. 1890

BOTTOM: A postcard showing the new Light tower, along with the keeper's house and covered walkway, c. 1910

Marblehead Light, Marblehead, Mass.

Author's Note

I remember the year clearly: 1996. I was a sitting Marblehead Selectman, and early that year, William J. "Spider" Healey, a popular, longtime letter carrier on the Marblehead Neck route, whispered in my ear that there was to be a 100th birthday on Marblehead Neck in April. Could I guess whose? Or what's?

Bill Conly in Marblehead Light's lens room, 2009

I hadn't a clue.

A few days later he solved the mystery: The Marblehead Light tower at Chandler Hovey Park would be 100 years old. A longtime avid student of the town's history, I didn't need to hear any more—I was off and running.

Maybe it was inevitable? I'm a 12th generation Marbleheader, so I probably came into the world with a love of history in my blood!

I discovered that there wasn't a lot of written information all in one spot about the Light. But I had already fallen hook, line, and sinker for that odd metal skeleton of a tower on Marblehead Neck. Nope, it wasn't lovely or charming the way a lot of traditional old New England lighthouses are. But during the long journey to uncover its past, I found that even without being pretty, Marblehead's Light tower (for a tower it is and not a "lighthouse" at all) was and is unique in all of New England—and, yes, beloved of the town. (In these pages, we'll refer to both Marblehead's older lighthouse and its light tower as the "Light.")

Over the years, I've given dozens of lectures on the Light's history and countless public and private tours up and down its 127 narrow, steep, winding stairs—including the 7-rung ladder at the top to the lantern room. From its height, dozens of people—both the merely curious and the passionate, avid lighthouse fans from everywhere—have seen that spectacular view out over Marblehead Harbor and Salem Sound. And what a view! (I remember once hanging back discreetly in the stairwell while a young man

TOP: A postcard showing Marblehead Harbor in deep
winter, 1907. The harbor froze in both 1907 and 1912
(and in several other years as well).

BOTTOM: A postcard, c. 1905, of the ferry dock off Front
Street. Ferry service to the Neck was popular and
continued into the 1960s.

Marblehead, Mass. · Frozen Harbor

Marblehead, Mass. Ferry Landing.

offered his earnest, top-of-the-Light marriage proposal.) The tours of the Light always had U. S. Coast Guard approval, but they finally came to an end amid concerns about liability. A few lucky souls still get the chance to climb up and catch the view today, including the Rotary Club of Marblehead crew (on the original inspiration of Jim Shay) who string up the decorative lights around the tower for the holidays.

Today, sophisticated electronic navigation has made lighthouses everywhere all but obsolete. Every year, the U. S. Coast Guard declares more of them surplus and either sells them to private owners or arranges to have them dismantled. I can't help but think that those that no longer stand have departed with some invaluable American history.

But until its own next era arrives, Marblehead Light will continue to shine out to sea as it has done for more than 180 years, offering both a welcoming light to incoming sailors and a reminder of days gone by.

Bill Conly, June 2017

About Bill Conly

When asked where his love of history comes from, Bill Conly always begins with his long family heritage. He might mention his job as a 12-year-old fare collector on the harbor ferryboat *Kelpie*, and his teenage years on the harbor when World War II's returning veterans became the Marblehead Transportation Company waterfront crew and Bill's earliest mentors. He could include his stint as assistant harbormaster on the town's police boat, and his stewardship of Marblehead's Corinthian Yacht Club in 2005-06 as commodore. And then the list might morph into a cascade of ancestral accomplishments: his uncle who was town fire chief; his paternal grandfather Frank E. Conly, a chairman of the Marblehead Board of Selectmen; and his maternal grandfather Arthur S. Adams, a state senator from Marblehead whose work paved the way for finally improving the causeway as a reliable road to the Neck in the early 1900s. And he would surely mention East Coast cruising aboard his beloved Nonsuch, *Mud Hen*.

Bill has lived his entire adult life in the same house in Marblehead, while working for 40 years in the insurance business and then running his own local insurance agency. He's a singular town cheerleader and activist, and it's a rare Marblehead town committee he hasn't served on.

Bill and his wife Renee raised three daughters—Rebecca, Jessica, and Rachel—all of whom now live in Maine. Bill continues his avid pursuit of Marblehead's robust history, with plans for more books about his hometown.

Town of Marblehead Historical Commission, August 2017

Early 20th-century yachting in Marblehead primarily featured sailing vessels. Boats "dressed ship" with nautical flags from masthead to bow and stern. All boats, regardless of size, used the Light (left) as a key aid to navigation.

Foreword

by Eric Jay Dolin

Marblehead Light is one of the town's most iconic symbols. It is incorporated into the logos of many local businesses, and no tour of the town would be complete without a stop at Chandler Hovey Park to gaze up at the tower or walk around its base. Whatever you might think about its aesthetic qualities, Marblehead Light is an integral part of the town's identity and its marvelously rich history.

Bill Conly, in this wonderfully written book, tells the fascinating story of Marblehead Light with skill and grace. That story, however, is only a small part of a much larger history of America's lighthouses, the brilliant beacons that have served our nation so well for more than 300 years.

America's first lighthouse was built on Little Brewster Island at the mouth of Boston Harbor, and was lit on September 14, 1716, inaugurating America's commitment to promoting navigational safety and encouraging the growth of maritime commerce. In the ensuing centuries, America built more than 1,000 lighthouses, draped like glistening pearls along the nation's vast coastlines, from New England to the Gulf of Mexico, the Great Lakes, and the Pacific Coast all the way to Alaska.

New England led the way. Of the ten lighthouses built in America before the American Revolution, seven were located along New England's shores. Hundreds more would follow, making New England one of the best-lit regions in the country. New England still boasts some of the nation's most beautiful and impressive lighthouses. These range from Portland Head Lighthouse in Maine, which draws more than one million visitors a year, to the soaring twin towers of Rockport's Thacher Island Lighthouse, to the stately mansion that is New London Ledge Lighthouse, located at the mouth of the Connecticut River.

Although Marblehead Light is not one of New England's most beautiful or impressive lighthouses, it is undeniably unique, as the region's only skeletal light tower. Such structures are far more common down south, especially along the Gulf coast, with the Coney Island Lighthouse in New York the closest to Marblehead. The uniqueness of Marblehead Light is very fitting because Marbleheaders themselves are unique. Like the Light, we stand out in a crowd.

But the Light is not Marblehead's only connection to America's enthralling lighthouse history. One of the most illustrious Marbleheaders, Elbridge Gerry, was instrumental in creating America's lighthouse establishment. Born and raised in Marblehead, Gerry served Massachusetts as both a representative in Congress and as governor, and would later go on to become vice-president under President James Madison. Although he is best known for his connection to the politically explosive term "gerrymandering," among his more notable and far less contentious contributions to American history was his introduction of the first draft of a bill that would transfer to the newly-formed federal government the management of all existing lighthouses. This bill, ultimately signed by President George Washington on August 7, 1789, not only

Marblehead Neck, near the Light, provided a perfect setting to view the visiting New York fleet, c. 1903.

placed the federal government in charge of all lighthouses, but also gave it the responsibility for lighthouse construction, operation, and maintenance from that point forward.

In introducing this bill, Gerry took a bold step, overcoming his own political inclinations. As a member of the Antifederalist Party, he opposed on principle a strong centralized national government, and many of his fellow antifederalists argued that lighthouses should remain under the control of state governments. But Gerry had grown up in one of the country's foremost fishing communities, and his family owned a fleet of ships that engaged in coastal and transatlantic trade; he knew how heavily mariners relied on lighthouses, and believed the federal government was in the best position to build and run them.

With GPS and all the other high-tech navigational equipment available today, lighthouses are not as critically important as they once were in safely guiding vessels along the coast. Nevertheless, mariners, especially local commercial and recreational boaters, still rely on lighthouses to provide a helpful and familiar means of navigation. And if the high-tech equipment fails, it's reassuring to know that lighthouses are still there. The majority of the roughly 700 lighthouses still standing in the United States continue to serve as active aids to navigation.

Marblehead Light is one of those steadfast and faithful beacons. How much longer her light will shine is anyone's guess. Every year, the U. S. Coast Guard decommissions more lighthouses. Many are transferred free of charge to local governments or non-profit organizations, while others are sold to private individuals. A few are demolished. Some of the transferred lighthouses remain lit, while others go dark.

The ultimate fate of Marblehead Light is an open question. If the Coast Guard decommissions Marblehead Light, the town has the right to claim ownership of the tower and the light. When that day comes, and it almost certainly will, I hope that the town steps forward to take on this responsibility. Marblehead just wouldn't be the same without its Light tower guarding the harbor's entrance and sending out a welcoming green beam to mariners in search of safe passage along an often unforgiving coast.

Eric Jay Dolin is the author of *Brilliant Beacons: A History of the American Lighthouse*; *When America First Met China: An Exotic History of Tea, Drugs, and Money in the Age of Sail*; *Leviathan: A History of Whaling in America*; and *Fur, Fortune, and Empire: An Epic History of the Fur Trade in America*. He lives in Marblehead with his family.

Detail from *View of Marblehead Neck in 1797*, by
Captain Samuel Stiness, 1797. This painting on a fireboard
shows Marblehead Neck devoid of any settlement.
The bucolic scene includes a simple cabin, water well,
and grazing livestock.

Chapter One

A New Light for Marblehead

It was the early 1800s and maritime commerce was thriving along the shores of New England. There was no question about the need for a lighthouse at Marblehead Harbor, Marblehead, Massachusetts.

Ship owners, skippers, and fishermen in Marblehead and in the waters of Salem Sound and beyond were eager champions for one—for protection from the hazardous rocky shoreline, the fluctuating winds, and the often-unpredictable weather. In his book, *Shipwrecks North of Boston, Vol. 1*, Marblehead author Ray Bates Jr. writes of hundreds of

shipwrecks that occurred in the waters off Salem and Marblehead. How many were the result of the poorly lit shoreline is undetermined; the lack of reliable, visible onshore or nearshore illumination surely played a significant role.

But … where could a lighthouse best be built? There were several possibilities.

On August 30, 1831, a Marblehead Town Meeting was convened to look at these possibilities. Townsman Eleazer P. Graves and others presented a proposal "to erect a Lighthouse on Point of Neck by the Government of the United States and to see if the Town assembled will petition Congress for that purpose." (*Marblehead Town Meeting Minutes*, August 30, 1831)

The town agreed to the proposal, but not everyone favored the proposed location. David Henshaw (1791-1852), collector of the Port of Boston and New England's area superintendent of lighthouses, opined that the light should be built at Fort Washington, a high point of land now called Fountain Park. Others thought the right spot was Gale's Head—today's Fort Sewall—at the harbor's mouth, while the town's fishermen and seagoing merchants, along with the powerful East India Marine Society in Salem, supported building the lighthouse at the tip of Marblehead Neck.

The dispute prompted Marblehead to take its usual course: in December of 1831, Town Meeting named a committee of town residents. Its members—Thomas Elkins, Nathaniel Adams, William

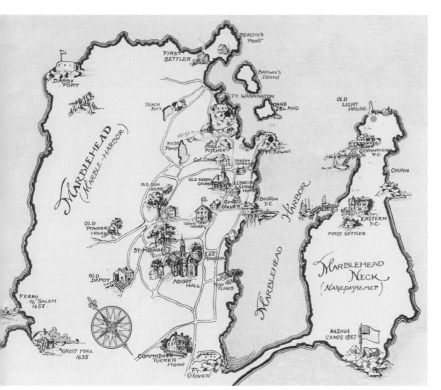

Detail of a map drawn in 1929 by Marian M. Brown included the three locations (shown here by two red dots and a green dot) considered by the town for the 1835 Marblehead Light.

LeCrew, Benjamin Wormstead, George Cloutman, David Blaney, John Dixey, and Richard Meek—were charged with providing advice to Congress about where the lighthouse should be built.

After giving attention to each site, the committee members were unanimous: locate the lighthouse at Point of Neck. "We have a good harbour and wish to make it easy access to the care worn and weather beaten mariner, so that he may find easily a haven of safety if not the haven of his desires," the group wrote (*Marblehead Town Meeting Minutes,* c. 1832). And despite Mr. Henshaw's opinions, the residents of Marblehead voted in 1833 to accept the committee's decision.

TOP: An early painting of Marblehead Light included its sturdy flagpole.
BOTTOM: An 1886 drawing by Charles A. Walker illustrates the variety of marine traffic that relied on the Light to provide safe passage in and out of port.

Dedicated to the Merchants of Boston, mezzotint by William Burgis, 1729, showing the original Boston Light and its armed British lighthouse tender. This lighthouse was deliberately burned by American patriots at the start of the American Revolution in order to keep British ships in the dark. In 1776, as the British fled Boston for Halifax, they blew up the charred lighthouse, in turn denying the Americans use of the navigational beacon. Americans rebuilt the lighthouse in 1783.

Marblehead's first lighthouse, built in 1835, would be far from the earliest on the New England coast. That honor went to Boston Light on Little Brewster Island in Boston Harbor, after many years of haranguing by ship owners, fishermen, and mariners who had struggled (often losing lives, ships, and cargo) against the ragged northeast coast. If their businesses—and indeed New England commerce—were to thrive, they needed much better and safer navigational markers than the rudimentary bonfires on hilltops and pots of burning oakum that served (poorly) to light up the coastline. It was during the 18th century that these early methods of illumination were replaced by oil lanterns. Following a petition to the Massachusetts General Court in 1713, Boston Light was first lit in the late summer of 1716.

A new committee was then named to begin the actual task of establishing the new lighthouse: John Ingalls, Edmund Bray, Richard Caswell, Francis Smith, and Peter Dixey Jr. went about procuring the needed land on the Neck, a parcel of 3.97 acres then owned by John W. Green and Ephraim Brown. After some dickering over the price, the land was conveyed to the town on August 10, 1833, for $375. The following June (1834), Congress appropriated $4,500 for the construction of a small lighthouse, a keeper's house, and additional outbuildings.

That same year, a traditional—if rather diminutive—white stone lighthouse with soapstone roof and lantern room was built. It stood from its base at 34 feet 6 inches above mean high water, with a total height of 23 feet 3 inches, making the focal plane (the

VIEW OF THE TOWN OF MARBLEHEAD, MASSACHUSETTS.

An 1854 engraving of Marblehead Harbor from *Gleason's Pictorial* shows fish flakes on Skinner's Point. The diminutive Light is visible on the far right.

point from which the light was produced) 57 feet 9 inches above mean high water. A ventilation aperture 28 inches square helped vent the smoke and heat generated by the oil lamps (in front of the reflectors).

At the same time, a dwelling was built for the Light keeper, along with a covered walkway to the lighthouse, a barn, a privy, a pump, a well, a boathouse, and a chicken coop. The roadway out to the Neck from town, via a rudimentary causeway, was not always passable due to storms, so a traditional 20-foot Grand Banks dory became the Light keeper's primary means of transportation. And, in keeping with the standard practice of the day for U. S. government-run lighthouses, the land was deeded by the town to the federal government on July 10, 1835. The following year, Marblehead reported a total construction expenditure for the Light and additional buildings of $3,946.93—well under the approved Congressional allotment.

New England native and former USS *Constitution* gunner Ezekiel Darling was named the Light's first keeper, for a yearly salary of $400. He would serve in the post for 25 years until he was 70 and nearly blind. (See Chapter Six for more on Darling and his fellow keepers.)

The Light first brightened the waters off Marblehead on October 10, 1835, and the picturesque stone building would stand as Marblehead's beacon for the next 61 years.

Marblehead artist J. O. J. Frost (1852–1928) devoted his final years to painting the Marblehead of his childhood. Many of his Marblehead Harbor images included the schooners that fished the Grand Banks and the Light on the Neck that guided them to and from port. This detail from *A Bird's Eye View in 1867* also illustrates how sparsely built the Neck was in the mid-1800s.

The Light in Marblehead Light

The notion of oil-fired lamps being visible far, far offshore begs the question: How was it possible? And how did ships' captains and mates know where they were when they did see the lamps? Logic points first to navigational skill; but an important second were the lighthouses that began appearing along the New England coastline through the 18th and 19th centuries. Some of these used single-lamp illumination, others used lamps in a series to produce more light.

The Argand lamp was first developed by a young Swiss physicist, Aimé Argand, whose invention featured a hollow cylinder within a circular wick that allowed air to flow both inside and outside the wick's flame. The added cylindrical glass chimney allowed a concentrated flow of air that kept the flame steady while eliminating side drafts. Argand patented this lamp in 1784, and it came into common use in both public and private buildings. Though various accounts differ, inventor Winslow Lewis was said to be the first to pair the Argand lamp with parabolic reflectors (picture the curved surface of a satellite dish). The apparatus consisted of ten whale-oil-burning Argand lamps, each outfitted with a parabolic reflector, which collected and reflected the light, capturing more of it and thus greatly enhancing it. But the Argand and Lewis lamps were far from perfect: Their glass chimneys sooted up quickly, the thin copper reflectors warped easily when heated, and the works required constant cleaning. The light produced was better, but still not visible more than about a dozen miles out to sea and still giving the great merchant vessels inadequate time to change course if conditions warranted.

Still, convinced by tests of the Lewis lamps at Boston Light and at Thacher Island, Congress passed legislation in March 1812 enabling the purchase of the Lewis lamp patent and ordering the lamp's installation in all American lighthouses (there were 49 at the time, and Lewis lamps were installed in 40 of them by December of 1812). And even after French scientist Augustin-Jean Fresnel had introduced his far superior reflecting lens in Europe (called the Fresnel lens, after its inventor)—to acclaim and broad adoption—the Lewis lamp remained the U. S. standard for some time. Its popularity finally began to wane in the mid-1800s as the first Fresnel lenses arrived in America and word spread rapidly about their unsurpassed brilliance.

BELOW: An illustration from an 1867 French publication *Les Merveilles de la Science* shows the Argand lamp's circular wick inside the glass chimney.

Fig. 10—Verre du bec d'Argand

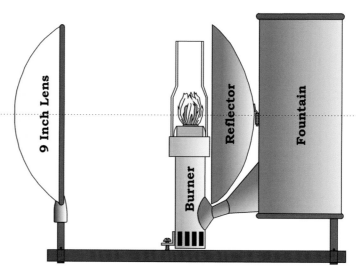

Winslow Lewis's original 1810 lamp with 9-inch reflector and 9-inch lens

Records show that Marblehead's first illumination in the Light was white, made possible by ten lamps with three-quarter-inch wicks—six lamps in a lower series and four in an upper, with each lamp accompanied by a reflector. This was the so-called Lewis lamp, fueled by whale oil, that could be seen many miles out to sea in clear weather.

Oddly, there was never any evidence of a fog signal at Marblehead Light, though these were common

TOP: An etching of Point of Neck by Kelburn Del, c. 1850, clearly shows a day marker on Marblehead Rock (at left). BOTTOM: Mrs. Isaac Fenno's 1875 painting shows the start of Marblehead Neck's building boom.

In 1819, Augustin-Jean Fresnel (pronounced freh-NELL), shown here, was commissioned by the French government to develop an improved lighting system for French lighthouses. Rather than the standard lantern flame with reflectors, Fresnel turned to glass lenses, using them to surround and greatly enhance the light produced by a flame—thus capturing even more of the light and projecting it outward. Author Terry Pepper writes: "In its simplest form, Fresnel's design was a barrel-shaped array of lenses encircling the light source. In the area immediately horizontal to the light source, *dioptric* lenses [prisms] magnified and concentrated the visible light as it passed directly through them. At the same time, above and below the light source, multiple *catadioptric* prisms mounted around the periphery of the barrel each collected and intensified the light and redirected it in the same plane as the *dioptric* lenses. With Fresnel's optic array, output was increased dramatically from the old reflector systems, with as much as eighty percent of the light captured..."

The Fresnel lenses projected light many miles farther out to sea. The lenses could be made in different sizes, or "orders," with a first-order lens the largest, nearly 12 feet high. The apparatus could be either fixed or rotating via a clockwork-like mechanism that enabled the intermittent signal flashes of light. And there was one other great advantage: the Fresnel lens could be built in one location and transported in sections to another, making assembly and modification in existing lighthouses far easier. The Fresnel was quickly adopted as the standard around the world, remaining so until well into the 20th century.

This illustration shows how the dioptric and the catadioptric prisms work in concert to reflect and refract the light rays into horizontal planes.

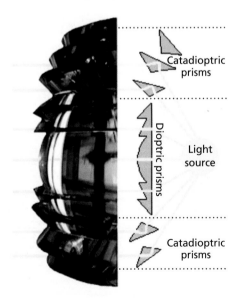

Catadioptric prisms

Dioptric prisms

Light source

Catadioptric prisms

FRESNEL ORDERS

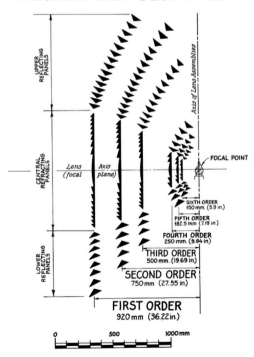

Oil painting of Elbridge Gerry, by William Goodwin in 1860

The U. S. Lighthouse Board, a federal department created in 1852 within the Department of Treasury, became responsible for the construction and maintenance of all lighthouses and navigation aids in the U. S. between 1852 and 1910. But much earlier, it was Marblehead's own Elbridge Gerry who, as a congressman in 1789, had first introduced the U. S. Lighthouse and Navigational Systems Bill (H.R. Bill 12). Passed by Congress on August 7, 1789, it was signed into law by President George Washington, effectively creating America's first public works program. This new governing body controlled all of America's lighthouses, beacons, and navigational bells and buoys. Like many such agencies, it went through alterations in name, mission, and leadership through the decades, as American seagoing commerce boomed and the lighthouses became ever more essential and strategic. (In 1939, the Lighthouse Service was finally absorbed into the brand-new U. S. Coast Guard.) In 1989, to commemorate the bicentennial of the lighthouse bill, President Ronald Reagan signed a bill designating August 7 (of that year only) as National Lighthouse Day. Then in 2013, the Senate passed a resolution making August 7 that year National Lighthouse Day; efforts are now underway to make August 7 a permanent commemorative day.

at other lighthouses, including the nearby lighthouse on Bakers Island, which was first lit in 1798.

Over the first half of the 19th century, Marblehead's Light (presumed to feature a Lewis lamp) was regularly cleaned, repaired, and updated. By 1896 when the new Light tower was built, it held what European lighthouse keepers considered the most technologically advanced lighting apparatus in the world: a Fresnel lens (see sidebar, left). For Marblehead, it was reportedly a sixth-order lens.

Meanwhile, the diminutive Light's days were numbered, as the land around it on Point of Neck began to undergo dramatic change.

This early photograph of Marblehead Light, c. 1875, shows a lightning rod atop the lens room.

Photographs, c. 1880, clearly show the diminished stature of the original Marblehead Light relative to the steadily increasing number of sizable houses being built around it.

Chapter Three

A Building Boom on Marblehead Neck

The town of Marblehead had purchased only a modest plot of land for its original Light in 1833 from Ephraim Brown. Brown's land holdings on the Neck had vastly increased over the years, until he owned some 250 acres, nearly the entire 300-acre area of the Neck. He had established a prosperous farm on the land by mid-century. But upon his death in the 1860s, the land was leased to other holders, one of whom was Martin Ham. Ham soon saw that land-leasing was more lucrative than farming, and he began in 1867 to under–lease building plots on the Neck to summer visitors, who in turn erected small summer cottages. As reported by Richard Whiting Searle in *Marblehead Great Neck* (1937), quoting an article from the *Commercial Bulletin* in 1870 in Boston: "The booths and cozy little shanties are in full bloom, dainty city damsels may be seen bereft of fashions folly [sic] and conducting themselves in a manner that would shock the sensitive nerves of a sojourner at Newport or Saratoga; and [the] stiff and stern pater familias frees

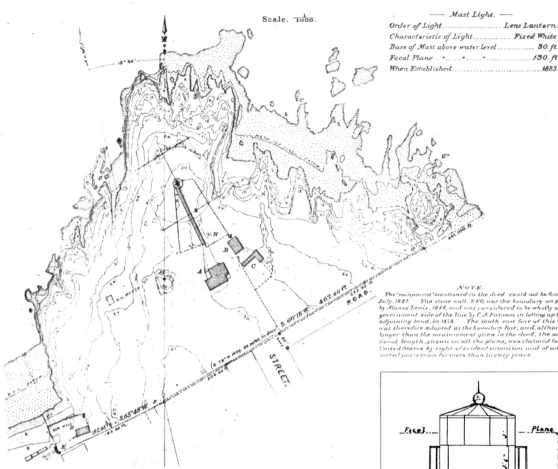

Scale, 1/1000.

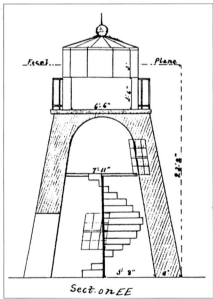

Sect. on EE

himself entirely from the meshes of his ledger and bank account, and roams about the Neck reveling in the freedom he encounters at every step."

Word had spread about the seaside pleasures of summering on the Neck and more visitors arrived, pitching commodious tents and remaining for the warmest months with their families. "In a few years," wrote Samuel Roads Jr., in his 1897 *History and Traditions of Marblehead*, "the ocean-side presented the appearance of an encampment of a small army. Hundreds of tents were pitched along the shore…and the dwellers found health and happiness in the calm enjoyment of their surroundings."

TOP: This blueprint, dated 1887, shows the location of Marblehead's original lighthouse, the mast added in 1883, the keeper's house, and several outbuildings.

INSET: A cutaway illustration of the 1835 Light includes dimensions.

It wasn't long before the Neck saw an influx of outside money and development. Starting in 1872, larger house lots were laid out and summarily sold at auction, and the smaller cottages gave way to lavish summer homes. A meetinghouse was built, as was Snow's Store on Harbor Avenue, containing a post office (Station 10, the Marblehead Neck branch), and a permanent summer community was born. The newly built Eastern (organized in 1870) and Corinthian (established in 1885) Yacht Clubs were bringing to Marblehead some of the greatest yachting fleets of the century, and an energetic ferry service commenced, transporting one and all from Marblehead across the harbor to the Neck.

TOP: A photograph of the Neck and the causeway, c. 1890, shows electric utility poles and farming but no buildings. BOTTOM: This old-time camp at Marblehead Neck, c. 1867, was located near the Neck's main ferry landing and what is now the Corinthian Yacht Club.

Ever-taller houses on the Neck, some with cupolas, eventually overpowered the original Light and its beam, c. 1880.

In the midst of this flurry of construction, the humble 23-foot stone lighthouse at the water's edge remained lit as it had for 50 years. But now, it became increasingly difficult for vessels approaching Marblehead Harbor to see: With the Neck's growing number of grand new houses, some of them built taller than the lighthouse itself, the Light's modest pinpoint illumination became obscured, rendering it nearly useless for those arriving in Marblehead Harbor by sea.

Frustrations among fishermen and sea captains grew, their complaints reflected in the U. S. Lighthouse Board reports of 1893 and 1894: "Many merchant vessels loaded with coal and general merchandise ply between this and other ports along the shore, and scores of yachts, with hundreds of pleasure seekers, make this their headquarters during the summer. The harbor, when not properly lighted, is difficult of approach, especially from the south. Mariners, ship owners, and others have complained for some years that the many dwellings lately built obscure the light. The difficulty has been partly overcome by showing a light from a lantern hoisted on a mast; but this is only a makeshift. The safety of commerce absolutely requires that a higher tower be erected. It is now proposed, therefore, to build a brick tower about 100 feet high, on the site of the present tower…."

As a partial remedy, a temporary 100-foot mast was erected in 1883, adjacent to the existing Light, with a nightly oil-burning lantern at its peak. Along with myriad other

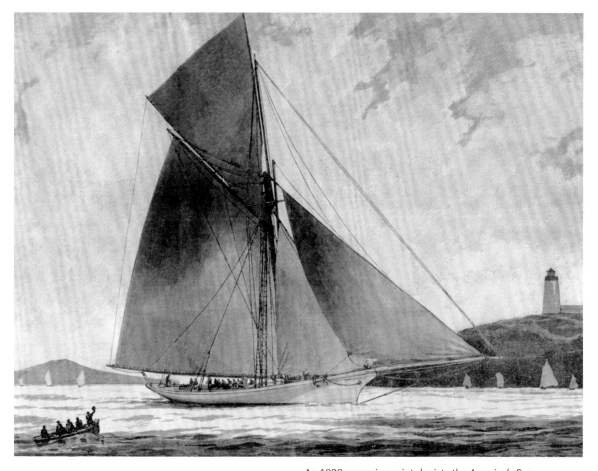

An 1890 magazine print depicts the America's Cup defender, *Volunteer*, sailing past Marblehead Light.

duties, the Light's keeper was now required to hoist the lantern, with its white light, up the mast every night, along with keeping the original Light lit and in good working order. Marblehead's lighthouse and mast soon became known as the "Twin Lights." (Twin lights were not uncommon then, and many were visible up and down the coast as early as the 1770s. Across Salem Sound from Marblehead, Bakers Island and Thacher Island—the closest to Marblehead—each boasted two substantial lighthouses.)

Despite its height, the mast lantern was far from ideal and quickly became a nuisance: the keeper would have to hoist the lantern up the mast each evening, often having to let it down for relighting when it blew out on the way up. Finally, thanks to the recommendation of the U. S. Lighthouse Board in 1893, a new 100-foot brick lighthouse was approved for the site at an estimated cost of $45,000. It would never be built.

The following year, the old stone lighthouse was condemned by the federal government and plans were made to dismantle it.

This photograph, c. 1905, shows the expansive array
of outbuildings around the keeper's house, including a
chicken coop and pens for livestock. Also visible here is the
covered walkway from the house to the new Light tower.

Keeping House at the Light

From its earliest days, there was indisputably far more to managing Marblehead Light than simply keeping its lamp wicks lit at dusk and extinguished at dawn. Keepers were responsible for maintaining detailed records of the supplies they used, along with the nearly endless task of keeping the Light clean and in good running order. There were glass chimneys, reflectors, and brass fittings to polish; lantern room curtains to be closed at daylight (to protect the lens) and opened at night; windows (inside and out) to clean daily; and the general area of the Light to be kept in pristine order.

And that didn't include the tasks of maintaining the keeper's quarters and outbuildings, livestock, subsistence garden, and covered walkway to the Light, with their constant needs for repair and replacement.

Indeed, the grounds included the house and boathouse, chicken coops, pens for cow, pigs, and goats, a privy, and eventually an oil house. The first of the Light's houses featured two rooms and a kitchen on the first floor and two bedrooms on the second. Like many of the older homes in Marblehead today, the basement housed a brick cistern, this one holding 2000 gallons of fresh water (town water was not piped to the Light until 1899). In 1867, the boathouse, pier, pump,

Mary Drayton (Dewey), dressed for winter, sits happily with her cat on the steps of the Light keeper's house, c. 1917.

Mary Drayton Dewey, daughter of Light keeper Henry Drayton, recalled growing up at the Light in the late 19th and early 20th centuries. The youngest of eight children of Henry and Mary Drayton—her father had been appointed keeper in 1893—she especially remembered the isolation in winter on the Neck. Although the summer visitors were plentiful, winter brought no one, with the nearest neighbor a half-mile away. But the keeper's house was "a cozy place," lit by kerosene lamps and with hot-water radiators in every room. There were two floors, with living room, dining room, kitchen, pantry, and parlor on the first, and four bedrooms and a bath on the second. "My father went to Boston once a month for supplies," she said, and returned with "barrels of flour and sugar and beans." There was a sizeable garden and her mother canned a lot of its harvest.

The government supply boat came twice a year with wicks and fuel oil for the lamp along with other supplies, and the visits became a "big occasion." Getting to school was a challenge; during the summer, the ferry made round trips to the Light, stopping at various landings along the way. But in the winter, the landings were pulled up and there was a mile walk to the only ferry landing on the Neck, and then another mile walk to school upon arrival at the town dock. Five of the Drayton children including herself were born at the Light. And when it came time for her mother to deliver, she would tell her boys that they should let the doctor know on their way to school. "The doctor would have to wait for low tide and then come over the causeway with his horse and buggy," Mary recalled. But there were few problems and very little sickness then. (*From a newspaper article kindly provided by Janet Drayton, granddaughter of Mary Drayton Dewey. Its date and source are unknown but are thought to be from the* Marblehead Messenger.)

and plank walkway between house and Light were repaired and improved. (Early photographs show a pier, gangway, float, and boathouse railway for the dory.)

An 1869 U. S. Lighthouse Board report noted: "The brick oven in the kitchen has been taken away and a closet built in its place, an iron sink set, two chimneys retopped, addition roof reshingled, and wall-paper for two rooms supplied. The walls of [the]

covered way have been clapboarded and [the] roof repaired; two window frames of the [Light] tower have been taken out and reset, packed with paint cement; the privy has been rebuilt, and that and [the] covered [walk]way whitewashed; a new ensign, and pipes and linings for stove, supplied." (The house was ultimately rebuilt in 1878.)

While a federal government supply boat would visit the Light twice a year for provisioning (and yes, there was the unreliable causeway road and the dory that could be rowed across the harbor to downtown Marblehead in an emergency), Marblehead Light families, already isolated from neighbors and friends, needed to be as self-sufficient as possible. Lighthouse children were either home-schooled or sent across the harbor by boat for classes, weather permitting. (The original rudimentary road across the causeway, once used principally to drive livestock over to the Neck for grazing, was often unusable.)

TOP: The Drayton's cow (cows were common on many properties at the time) was a source of fresh milk.
INSET: Care for Marblehead Light and its compound kept the keeper and his family fully occupied throughout the year. Postcard detail, c. 1910

These two photographs from early 1896 show the construction of the new Marblehead Light tower, erected in the same location as the old Light. The new Light's center cylinder (containing the spiral stairway) was assembled from sections built in Virginia and shipped north via train. The new lantern room sat atop scaffolding (on left in both photographs) while the temporary lantern-on-a-mast was still in use, both shining a light each evening. The covered walkway was cut back from the Light's base, most likely to facilitate construction.

Chapter Five

A Light Tower for Marblehead

By 1895, with the original Light deemed completely insufficient as a navigational aid, the call went out for bids for building the government-approved new lighthouse at Marblehead. The old lighthouse was summarily demolished and a wooden scaffold erected to support a new lantern room while the Light tower was under construction in the early months of 1896.

Bids came in for the construction of the new Marblehead Light and ranged widely, from $8,786 to $20,584. On July 22, 1895, the federal government chose the firm of Chamblin, Delaney & Scott of Richmond Virginia, with the new Light slated for building at $8,786, the lowest bid. The new foundation was poured on December 12, 1895.

But it would, after all, anchor no traditional New England rounded brick lighthouse that Marbleheaders anticipated—the kind that commonly peppered the East Coast. (Recall that the price for a traditional brick lighthouse had been estimated at $45,000.)

Instead, there emerged an impressive iron pyramidal skeleton, manufactured in Richmond and shipped north to be assembled on the exact site of the first Marblehead Light. The new tower was 100 feet high to the focal plane (the point of light) with polygonal sides, and, including the roof and ventilation shaft, it stood 134.6 feet above mean high water (U. S. Lighthouse Board original drawings, June 28, 1895). The spiral stairway, with its 127 steps inside the iron cylinder, took the keeper to the watch room and then a ladder of 7 steps brought him to the lens/focal plane, in the lantern room. There was a double door from the watch room to the outside catwalk and another small door out of the lantern room to a second, higher catwalk. A ladder connected the two catwalks outside. The covered walkway was re-built between the Light and the keeper's quarters.

In essence, the open-work structure consisted of eight vertical supports, or pilings, that leaned inward toward the top, and rested at ground level on eight concrete foundation

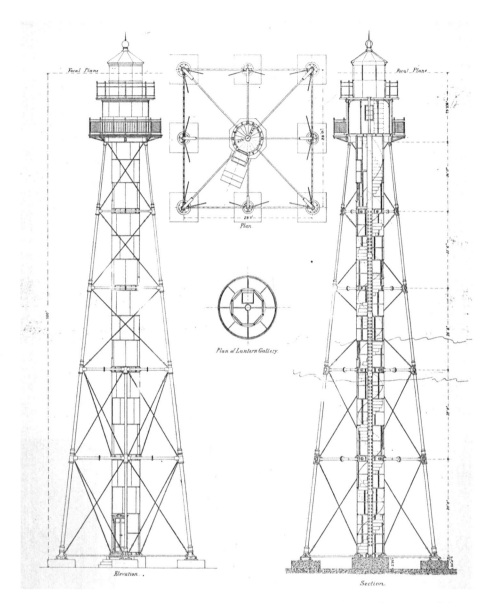

Focal Plane

Plan

Plan of Lantern Gallery

Elevation

Section

Marblehead's skeletal Light tower was in good company in America, although it was, and remains, the only such light tower in New England. While most towers today are listed (incorrectly) as "lighthouses" and are of various designs, they are light towers whose distinguishing features are the central cylinder inside of an outer open-iron framework featuring vertical "legs" that anchor and stabilize the structure. In the late 19th and early 20th centuries, these light towers were increasingly popular with Congress because they cost less than half the price of the more traditional stone or brick lighthouses, and they could be built much more quickly. Several of these towers survive in the U. S. and can be found along the Atlantic coast—from New York and New Jersey to Florida—and on the Great Lakes. Many others were destroyed by weather or demolished for safety reasons.

A copy of one page of the 1895 Light tower blueprints

platforms set in a square, with the pilings stabilized by alternating horizontal iron beams. The effect was a tall, spidery tower through which wind and water could freely blow without the resistance of hard-surface stone or brick.

The new tower was painted a dull brown. Here was its careful description: A "base coat of red lead ground in linseed oil, once sufficiently dried, two coats of 'Prince's Metallic Brown' paint ground in linseed oil will be added. The gallery railing, the parapet and lantern are to be painted with two coats of black. The interior surfaces are to be painted with three coats of white lead paint and the stairs of black."

When the new Light was lit on April 17, 1896, the old makeshift lantern-on-a-mast was dismantled.

When lit, Marblehead's 1896 Light shone with a white light using a sixth-order Fresnel lens.

Was it beautiful? Perhaps, to some. But as the *Marblehead Messenger* described it in an April 24, 1896, article: "The new light tower at Point Neck, though not adding to the picturesqueness of the Point, has demonstrated itself vastly more effective than the old one in the duty it was intended for. It was lighted last Friday night ...."

Nearly 50 years later, author Edward Rowe Snow, in his 1945 *Lighthouses of New England*, put it more delicately: "Of course it is to be realized that lighthouses are for utility and not for beauty, but in this case [in Marblehead], it is especially unfortunate that beauty and utility were not combined."

BELOW: The second Marblehead Light keeper's house, built in 1878. The temporary 100-foot mast, erected in 1883, dwarfs the man and the Light.

INSET: Fashionable young men pose next to the original Marblehead Light, c. 1890. Its years of service would soon come to an end.

Chapter Six

Marblehead's Wickies

From afar, New England's functioning lighthouses appeared to operate seamlessly and smoothly. But until well into the 20th century they could not run at all without ... people! Hardworking people who, for the most part, spent love and labor on the lights, and brought expert knowledge and great care—and not infrequently their families—to their lighthouse duties.

These were the storied "wickies" of the time—so named for the wicks they kept trimmed and in whale oil to keep the lantern flames burning brightly. While today's remaining lighthouses are lit automatically and without the labors of keepers (and a number still serve as navigational aids, alongside GPS), the lights of bygone days depended on the services of their keepers. And like all human endeavors, there were varying degrees of dedication to the work. Some wickies threw themselves into it, maintaining their lights and properties with iron will, and some simply found that lighthouse-keeping was not to their taste at all. For those who took the job seriously, lighthouse-keeping typically became a wholehearted family affair, with spouses and children living and working in and knowing a good deal about the lighthouses.

This was abundantly true for the Marblehead keepers too, starting with the first Light on the Neck in 1835.

In those years, the Light was still relatively isolated from Marblehead proper, connected only by a rudimentary road from town to Neck (now the Marblehead Neck causeway) that often

washed out in storms; boat transport across the harbor may have been infrequent but was more reliable. The keepers' families planted subsistence gardens and kept livestock for their own consumption, since major supplies came to the Neck by government boat only twice a year (and not always reliably, at that). But for many keepers and their wives and children, keeping the Light in good working order was the first order of family business.

For wickie families, the traditional 18th and 19th century division of labor by gender was frequently upended. Wickie wives cooked, cleaned, cared for children, and undertook the domestic chores. But when the keeper was ill or needed to be away, wives and families were expected to step up and take over the lighthouse duties. Some actually took over the permanent duties of light keeper if a husband or father died on the job. And increasingly, women were taking the keeper's job on their own. Indeed, the U. S. Lighthouse Board appeared to be quite comfortable appointing women keepers, deeming them especially worthy and capable of performing well. Marblehead itself welcomed one of the first, Jane Clemmons Martin, in 1860.

TOP: A spoon manufactured by Daniel Low and Company, Salem, Massachusetts, featuring Marblehead Light, c. 1880
MIDDLE: A U. S. Lighthouse Service brass oil-lamp feeder, issued to Marblehead's Light keepers, c. 1890
BOTTOM: An original iron key used for Marblehead's 1835 lighthouse door

Contrary to romantic lore about light-house-keeping, the duties of any keeper constituted a far greater load than simply making sure the wicks were lit and the light didn't go out during the night. There was hard labor: those wicks needed to be trimmed daily to remove burned sections; oil for the lamps had to be hauled up into the lantern room; and the entire mechanism of the Light—from lamps to reflectors, to glass chimneys, to brass fittings, to Fresnel lenses (once they were introduced)—had to be kept spotless and pristine, as did the windows enclosing the lantern room inside and out. And there were records to be kept daily as well—on weather conditions, shipwrecks, supply inventories, structural conditions, visitors, and other observations of the keeper. The family's dory needed to be kept in good repair, windows in all build-

Marblehead's first lighthouse keeper, Ezekial Darling, painted in China, 1811

ings and structures underwent constant repair, and the repainting of the buildings was a persistent duty. The twice-yearly government inspections to which all lighthouse keepers were subject were reason enough to be as thorough as possible (and yes, they looked at everything!). When lighthouses became electrified, the keeper's workload lessened considerably, but it was still a very demanding job.

Marblehead's own wickies carried many of the family names familiar to today's Marbleheaders: Bailey, Darling, Drayton, Goodwin, Martin. Their descendants remain town fixtures.

Details about Marblehead's wickies vary widely, from extensive to minimal. Some wickie families kept good records of their ancestors through the years, and others did not. Here, we share what we know. (The wickies' terms of service are in parentheses after their names.)

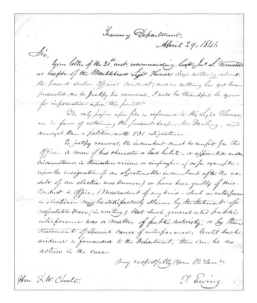

ABOVE: Ewing's 1841 letter stating that keeper Darling would not be removed from Marblehead's lighthouse service
BELOW: An 1801 watercolor of the schooner *Raven*, captained by Ambrose Martin, father of wickie Jane Clemmons Martin

Ezekiel Darling (1835–1860)

Darling was Marblehead's very first keeper, a veteran gunner's mate on the USS *Constitution*. He had also been an active privateer, serving on several of the vessels for which Marblehead was noted.

Darling had first gone to sea at eight or nine, and had later been wounded in the War of 1812. For the princely sum of $400 a year, he managed the Light from its first illumination in 1835 until 1860. As described in a newspaper article of 1857, Darling was a "man of small stature, but of a wiry and well-knit frame, showing that when in his prime he must have been capable of great endurance ...." Darling was said to have taken part in several rescues of shipwrecked mariners.

When engineer I. W. P. Lewis inspected the Light in 1842, Darling complained about the station's leaky tower, sweating lantern, and dampness in the house. Still, Lewis had nothing but praise for Darling in his 1843 report, writing: "Perfect order, cleanliness, and apparent comfort reign throughout the whole establishment, much to the credit of the keeper." (Courtesy Lighthousefriends.com)

A steady and reliable keeper, Darling was also handy and made several improvements to his home, reporting that

he had "floored" part of the basement and opened a passageway underneath the kitchen where the household's coal could be safely stored and kept dry. He had also built a porch on the north side of the house.

After many years of Darling's service at Marblehead Light, the U. S. Lighthouse Board, under the U. S. Secretary of the Treasury, received a letter requesting that Captain J. S. Wormstead replace Darling. At the same time, there was also on record a petition with 531 signatures in favor of retaining Darling as the keeper. On April 29, 1841, T. Ewing of the U. S. Lighthouse Board wrote a letter rejecting Darling's replacement and he continued as keeper. But toward the end of his service, Darling's eyesight began to fail and he was soon unable to perform his duties. He finally resigned after 25 years at the Light when permanent blindness set in. (In 1962, during repairs he made to the Light, Marbleheader Linc Hawkes placed a plaque on the door of the Light tower acknowledging Darling's long years of service, and noting—incorrectly and to the amusement of many in Marblehead— that Darling had served on the "USS *Constellation*.")

Jane Clemmons Martin (1860–1862)

Jane Clemmons Martin was one of ten children born to Ambrose and Elizabeth (Clemmons) Martin. Her father was keeper of the Bakers Island Light for 25 years, retiring in 1850.

A drawing of the mouth of Marblehead Harbor showing buildings on Cat Island (now known as Children's Island), c. 1860. During this time, Jane Clemmons Martin served as the wickie at Marblehead Light (at right). She grew up in a lighthouse family, learning the keeper's responsibilities from her father.

Martin's modern-day descendant, Marge Gallo Armstrong of Marblehead, has written that Martin lived with her parents and two siblings in Salem. Sometime before 1860, she had moved to East Boston to live with her brother Elbridge Gerry Martin and his children,

TOP: Detail from a painting by M. White of Marblehead Light, c. 1865, showing the Neck's hazardous shoreline. Mariners were grateful to have a guiding beacon at the harbor's entrance.

BOTTOM: A man, c. 1870, standing atop Marblehead Light, facing the ramshackle keeper's house, which was replaced in 1878

presumably to help out with the motherless family (Martin, the father of five, had become a widower in 1852). She was an "independent and adventurous woman," wrote Armstrong.

Martin replaced Ezekiel Darling on the Light in 1860, and became the only New England female light keeper of her time, although dozens more would follow at lighthouses elsewhere. She had learned her keeper's duties well, at the knee of her father, Captain Ambrose Martin of Marblehead, the Bakers Island Lighthouse keeper. And once appointed, she tackled the job with energy. Her work, like that of other keepers of the time, was to haul the night's supply of oil up the 134 steps (127 steps plus 7 ladder rungs) every morning to fill the lamp well, polish the lens, and make sure the protective canvas curtains were drawn tightly closed to protect the lens from the daytime sun. At dusk, she would climb the stairs again to fire the Light, and then extinguish it at dawn.

Martin, wrote Armstrong, had "quite an adventure at the lighthouse…the schooner *Mary E. Hiltz* had gone ashore on Marblehead Neck during a Sunday night snowstorm. Her captain had mistaken Marblehead Light for the Eastern Point Light and the schooner was totally wrecked. One of the crew, Thomas Christopher of Newfoundland, was drowned. The six remaining crew members remained on the wreck until Monday morning," when they made their way to shore and to the lighthouse. Martin made them as comfortable as possible, and the body of Christopher was recovered two days later and buried following a funeral service.

Martin never married and died in Boston on November 22, 1871. (Courtesy of Jane Clemmons Martin descendant Marge Gallo Armstrong, *Marblehead Musings* website)

John Goodwin (1862–1872)
Goodwin provided ten years of service at the Light, though the historic record contains no information about his tenure.

TOP TWO: The badge issued to U. S. lighthouse keepers and proudly worn on their dress uniforms. This one dates from the 1920s. Also shown is a button from keeper Henry Drayton's uniform, c. 1920.

BOTTOM: A postcard of the Marblehead Light tower property, c. 1910

James Scobie Bailey (1872–1892)

James S. Bailey, a former cabin boy who had sailed the Grand Banks, served as Marble-head's wickie for 20 years. He married Martha M. Brown of Marblehead, and fathered six children. It was during Bailey's tenure that the Light keeper's house was finally, despite many repairs, demolished and replaced by a larger two-story wood-frame house in which the Bailey family took up residence in 1878. (Martha Bailey Woodfin, the great-great granddaughter of James Bailey, still lives in Marblehead at this writing.)

Among the stories of Bailey's tenure was one reported in a *Boston Globe* article from 1889, in which Bailey was said to have saved more than a dozen people from waters near the Light. Another story noted that Bailey had also saved six men "as they clung to the rigging of their schooner during a winter gale, injuring himself in the process when his own boat was thrown by the violent waves. He managed to bring the men to the light-house, where he cared for them for several days. When Bailey requested that the affluent Philadelphian owners of the schooner reimburse him for the men's food, he was coldly informed that nobody had ordered him to feed them."

On another occasion, Bailey spied a boat in trouble in the harbor. By the time he launched his dory and rowed out to it, one of its occupants was already in the water. According to the *Boston Globe*, the man's "bald pate was all that could be seen," when Bailey dove in and pulled the man to safety.

A Marblehead postcard, c. 1880, shows the new keeper's house with its ornate trim at the eaves. A flagpole is visible on the far side of the covered walkway.

This time Bailey's courage earned him a medal from the Massachusetts Humane Society.

But Bailey wanted no medals and declared he would not accept any money for saving a life: "It is a duty for me to save my fellow men, and as long as I am able to wield an oar and keep my eyesight, I shall never refrain from undertaking the trip over the waves that may be the means of saving life." (Courtesy of Lighthousefriends.com)

TOP LEFT: Henry Drayton with his wife and daughter (both named Mary), c. 1917, on the steps of the Marblehead keeper's house

TOP RIGHT: Mother and daughter proudly raise a four-star flag on the staff next to Marblehead Light. The stars signified the four Drayton sons serving in WWI Armed Forces.

BOTTOM: A snowdrift dwarfs the Marblehead keeper's house, c. 1910.

Albert M. Hortey (1892–1893)

Hortey was assistant keeper at Boston Light before being transferred to Marblehead. He served for just five months and then returned to Boston Light as the keeper in May of 1893.

Henry Thomas Drayton (1893–1928)

Henry Drayton, the former mate of the U. S. Supply Steamer *Verbens*, took over the old Light in 1893 and was the first keeper of the new Light in 1896. He and his family lived in the keeper's house and, thanks to Drayton's trove of photographs, there is a wealth of historic images from his 35 years at the Light. (See daughter Mary Drayton Dewey's

Henry Drayton's 1918 Coastwise Identification Card reveals that he was a naturalized United States citizen, with "tatoo right arm," who owned the vessel *Art*.

recollections of life at the Light on page 36.) Described in a news article upon his retirement in 1928, he was a "somewhat thin man, weather-browned, slightly under normal height. With keen blue eyes, a close-cropped reddish mustache [and] the manner of a person who has learned speech with many and different species of man." He wore the navy-blue uniform and visored cap of the lighthouse service, and conducted many tours up the Light's long flight of steps to the watch room. After he retired he would relate some of his adventures on the Light, from the infamous March 29, 1899, grounding of the freighter *Norseman* and Drayton's assistance in the rescue of its crew (the Marblehead Humane Society, Station 10, in those days a marine rescue society, had led this rescue), to the lost stranger who appeared out of the fog one night, having struggled onto the Neck from his abandoned but anchored boat in high seas. Drayton rowed him out to the boat in the howling weather and together they managed to maneuver it through the wild wind and water to a safe haven in the harbor.

During World War I, the Light's boathouse was equipped with a telephone and became the living quarters for soldiers keeping watch on the coast. Drayton enjoyed the phone for a time once the military departed, but ultimately lost it during the changeover to electricity. It was under Drayton's watch that the Light color changed from white to ruby red, probably around 1922. He also oversaw the change in Light fuel from whale oil to electricity.

Russell B. Eastman (1928–1930)

The historic record contains no information on the service of this wickie.

Edwin C. Rogers (1930–1938)

Edwin "Sparkie" Rogers served for eight years at the Light, and he and his wife Hibernia raised their family in the keeper's cottage. Their daughter Barbara Rogers Mace (who, along with her older brother, was born at the Light, and, according to her husband Alan, grieved when the Light keeper's cottage was finally demolished in 1959) attended high school in Marblehead. The Rogers descendants still live in Marblehead. Sparkie Rogers resigned his wickie post on July 1, 1938, just one month before the massive and infamous hurricane of 1938.

As the Marblehead story goes, during Sparkie Rogers's time as keeper, his young son Edwin went missing at the Light, and a search ensued. Soon the

TOP: Sparkie Rogers, c. 1930
BOTTOM: In 1931, Marbleheaders welcomed the USS *Constitution* back to port for the first time since 1814, when she had taken refuge from British war ships. In 1814 there was no lighthouse to assist the Marblehead crewmen aboard the *Constitution* who piloted the ship into the harbor. INSET: A ticket issued to tour the ship in 1931. The *Constitution* visited Marblehead again in 1997.

boy was spotted atop the Light tower, perched on the ventilator bail (that portion of the topmost ventilator where hot gases are exhausted from a gas-burning lamp while keeping out wind-blown moisture). Rogers quickly made his way up to retrieve Edwin, and the story became Edwin's favorite childhood memory (doubt-less not shared by his mother and father!).

After serving as a wickie, Rogers went to work as a signal man for the Salem railroad.

Harry S. Marden (1938–1941)

Marden had no idea that within a few months of his appointment as keeper, he would join the ranks of the most celebrated Marblehead Light keepers.

On September 21, 1938, a hurricane dubbed the "Long Island Express" roared up the East coast, flattening trees and buildings with winds of 120 to 180 miles an hour. It killed 600 in New England and wrought damage to the tune of $400 million. The North Shore of Massachusetts suffered especially, with nearly $1 million in damages to the Marble-head yachting fleet alone.

Harry Marden watched the Light dim in the wind and knew that his work was going to be cut out for him that fateful fall night. But where would a fresh source of power come

Mariners and other visitors to the Neck in the 1950s were among the last to see a keeper's house alongside the Light.

from for the faltering Light? With electric power failing all over New England, Marden needed to act fast. The story is legendary in Marblehead: Marden drove his car up to the Light tower, hooked up the car's battery to the tower wiring, and kept the Light glowing all night. Then up he went into the watch room to spend the night in perhaps the most terrifying and vicious weather assault in his career. He tended the Light without a break until morning. It never went out.

Marden went on to serve the Light for four years, including one year during World War II when the Army again—as it had in World War I—occupied the Light. It stayed off-limits to the public for five years, from 1941 to 1946, while Marden returned to active military duty.

Though his tenure was relatively short, Marden's spot in Marblehead Light history remains firmly cemented, thanks to the great storm of 1938.

Joseph Barry (1947–1954)

Joseph Barry was Superintendent of Parks. He and his wife Beryl lived in the Light keeper's house and tended a beacon that was now powered by electricity; it did not require the rigorous attention and servicing of old. They were the last to occupy the house before it was razed.

The Marblehead Light tower stood tall amid the continuing building boom both on the Neck and in the area surrounding Fort Sewall, c. 1920.

Chapter Seven

From Whale Oil to Electricity, and Other Changes

By 1899, long-needed improvements were being made to the Light's outbuildings, including newly piped-in town water. A new brick oil house was built in 1907 just to the southwest of the Light tower, with a capacity of some 450 gallons in metal cans.

In 1910, the Light underwent a formal Department of Commerce and Labor inspection. All was found to be in good working order. Records show that sometime between 1910 and the next inspection in 1927—likely around 1922, although there was no apparent recorded date—the Light's emitted color was changed from white to ruby, specifically, "Type D ruby." The records of other lighthouses showed that changing the color of a light might be necessary when there were several lighthouses near each other in one area and color could help to distinguish them; or a red light might signify nearby dangers in the

sea (rocks just beneath the surface, for example). But there is no definitive explanation in the historical record for why Marblehead Light's color was changed.

And there was more: on August 1, 1922, the Light underwent a major fuel change from oil to electricity. That meant a change to the lantern itself: now it featured an electric light bulb of 150 watts, instead of an oil-burning lamp. It still emitted its traditionally bright glow—but always with an oil lamp held in reserve!

The electric bulb was the same 150-watt brightness that had been designed for light-ships. Then in the late 1930s (records suggest 1938), the Light's steady ruby color was altered again, this time to a steady green. There was local speculation about this—that any boat returning to Marblehead Harbor should have a green signal light on the left, or port, side. If the mariner's rule of "red right returning" held, then a green light in a lighthouse on the port side would indeed have made sense. Otherwise, there is no record of why the light was changed from ruby to green, where it remains to this day. (In New England today there are only two other lighthouses showing a green light: Fort Point Light, now in private hands, in New Castle, New Hampshire, shows a steady green; and Block Island's southeast lighthouse on Mohegan Bluffs produces a rotating green—it's now the property of the private Block Island Southeast Lighthouse Foundation.)

The Light's adjacent buildings underwent change again too, with the roof now gone from the walkway between the house and Light, though the wooden plank walkway remained. The old basement cistern was no longer in use,

At the turn of the 20th century, the keeper's dory remained a key means of transportation between Neck and mainland. The dory shed (the white building), located in the cove adjacent to the Light, provided storage.

thanks to the piped-in town water, and a new 13-foot dory graced the pier. In 1907 a brick oil house was added and still stands today, the only remaining building on the Light grounds; and the old boathouse was finally removed in January of 1930 to King's Neck at the west end of the Cape Cod Canal.

In October of 1927, and again in May of 1931, in Department of Commerce and Labor inspections, the Light and its buildings were found to be in good working order. Further needed improvements came in 1937, when the Light keeper's cottage and outbuildings were renovated and the surrounding wooden fence was replaced with a chain-link fence. Two years later, the Light tower was placed under the control of the U. S. Coast Guard.

By 1940, the Light grounds were temporarily graced by a Bilby Tower, one of two erected in Marblehead by the U. S. Coast and Geodetic Survey. Traditional survey methods, using stable instruments, required a steady, clear line-of-sight between survey points, uninterrupted by hills and trees. The high towers served these purposes well in determining land boundaries, toward improving transportation and navigation safety. Today surveyors rely on GPS and satellites for this purpose.

In 1956, Marblehead's Edward H. Goodwin, the chief engineer of all lighthouses in U. S. Coast Guard District 1, contracted with the Marblehead firm W. C. Peach Contractors to replace the Light's foundation footings beneath its eight pilings, apparently a significant undertaking. (In November of that year, Marblehead's Board of Selectmen proposed in a letter to the U. S. Coast Guard that the framework of the Marblehead Light tower be painted white; the proposal was summarily denied.)

Marblehead Light's Fixed Color Through the Years

 1835

 1896

 c. 1922

 1938

 1941-1946

 1946

BELOW: In 1940, a re-usable steel Bilby Tower, comprised of hundreds of interlocking parts, was temporarily erected next to Marblehead Light.

A bird's-eye view of the sturdy Light tower and Point of
Neck during Marblehead's 1938 Race Week. A day marker
(removed in 1954) can be seen on Marblehead Rock (at left).

Chapter Eight

The Light, the Wars, and the Government

During World War I, the Light's boathouse was converted to living quarters for the Navy; there were sailors in the Light standing watch and others patrolling the beaches. While a bit young to be romantically enthused about the boys in uniform, Mary Drayton Dewey (daughter of the Light keeper of the time, Henry Drayton) remembered that the sailors provided some "diversion at the Light," and might occasionally come to the house to play cards.

HARBOR VIEW, MARBLEHEAD, MASSACHUSETTS

ABOVE: Chandler Hovey was an avid yachtsman known for skippering many boats to victory, including the J Class *Yankee* (left, c. 1930). For decades Hovey sailed with family and friends serving as crew, including in the prestigious America's Cup trials. Though he sailed in six America's Cup defender series, he never won the honor of defending the Cup. LEFT: A plaque made in honor of Chandler Hovey's gift to the town

The Light went dark during World War II, when the military—this time the Army—again took control of the tower, and between 1941 and 1946 kept watch for wartime encroachments along coastal New England; military patrols along Marblehead's beaches were a common sight again, too. The Light was relit after the war, in 1946.

During Marblehead's Town Meeting of March 1947, voters agreed to accept the deed from the federal government conveying to the town a portion of the Light's land—minus the immediate area on which the Light stood—for which they would spend $5,000. But accepting the deed and approving the expenditure were two different things, and the voters hesitated. An abutter to the land, a resident named Chandler Hovey, approached the Marblehead Selectmen about the purchase, and encouraged them to approve it and

TOP: A watercolor by Samuel H. Bryant depicting a 38-foot wooden picket boat during sea trials near the Neck. During WWII, the James E. Graves boatyards, located in Marblehead, produced more than 136 boats for the U. S. Coast Guard, including 64 picket boats.

BOTTOM: By 1959, the Marblehead Light keeper's house looked aged and forlorn. It was torn down that year.

spend the money (perhaps as much to preserve it for the town as to preserve his own view!). But the selectmen balked. Hovey then appeared at a subsequent Town Meeting with a check in hand for $5000, which he gave the selectmen outright for the land purchase. The voters approved the purchase in October, and the government conveyed 3.74 acres of the land to Marblehead for park use. The area would later be named Chandler Hovey Park.

Since 1996, the sight of Marblehead Light aglow with festive strings of lights has become an anticipated part of December and July Fourth holiday celebrations.

Chapter Nine

The Historic Light Is Rededicated

In 1959, the Light keeper's house was razed—signaling the end of an era—and Marblehead Light became fully automated in 1960. Its Fresnel lens had long since been replaced by a modern 150-watt bulb accompanied by its 300mm lens and pairs of prisms that still emitted a steady green light equivalent in strength and brightness to the old sixth-order Fresnel. Today, there is a small 250-watt bulb in the Light, with four other bulbs held in reserve, should one fail. Oversight of the Light tower has remained within the Marblehead Harbormaster's office (which assumed its management in 2010), with ultimate responsibility for all lighting operations continuing under the care and oversight of the U. S. Coast Guard.

On June 15, 1987, the Light was added to the official National Register of Historic Places (number #87001479 under Lighthouses of Massachusetts Thematic Group). It was sandblasted in 1992 and repainted its traditional metallic brown.

For the first time, on July 4, 1996, and with Coast Guard approval, the Rotary Club of Marblehead (thanks to Jim Shay's leadership) decorated the Light top to bottom with an array of brightly colored lights. The decorations were repeated again the following Christmas, and the holiday traditions have continued to this day.

As part of Marblehead's 350th celebration (begun in 1999) of the town's founding, Marblehead Light was honored during a formal rededication and remembrance ceremony in early September 2002. The U. S. Coast Guard contributed by sponsoring speaking engagements by Rear Admiral Vivien Crea, then Commander of the First Coast Guard District, and Captain Daniel May, Commander Coast Guard Group Boston. They were accompanied by a contingent of enthusiastic sailors and a flotilla of boats in the harbor. The town's historical reenactment group, Glover's Marblehead Regiment, attended and marked the occasion with ceremonial musket salutes.

Said Admiral Crea in her address: "Not only do lighthouses provide a very practical service as aids to navigation for ships at sea, they serve as symbols of our rich maritime heritage and add to the splendor of our remarkable New England coastline….The lighthouses seem to touch the emotional core of every person who takes a moment to study the

TOP PHOTOGRAPHS: In 1992, Marblehead Light was scaffolded, wrapped, sandblasted, and repainted metallic brown.
BOTTOM LEFT: A 1996 cartoon by Marty Riskin celebrating Marblehead Light's 100th birthday.
BOTTOM RIGHT: The Marblehead Light logo designed by Lou Rugiullo, with a postage stamp of the other Marblehead (Ohio) lighthouse.

ABOVE and TOP RIGHT: Glover's Marblehead Regiment joined in the 2002 celebration of the town's 350th anniversary ceremonies at the Light, offering a processional and musket salute.

RIGHT: Plaques at Chandler Hovey Park commemorate Marblehead Light; one outlines its timeline and the other lists its wickies.

structure's lines, observe the light, or listen to its fog signal. During my short tenure as the First District Commander, I have developed a richer understanding of just how special lighthouses are to New England. For those who may not know, I have the privilege today of residing in the quarters of Hospital Point Light in Beverly. Being able to climb the lighthouse tower, admire the Fresnel lens and survey the seascape are memories that will always be with me."

In honor of the day, the U. S. Postal Service in Marblehead sponsored a first-day postage cancellation at the Marblehead Yacht Club, featuring a Marblehead Light logo designed by postal employee Lou Rugiullo. A bronze plaque written by this author—a gift of Marblehead's 350th Anniversary Committee—was installed near the Light describing its history.

On May 29, 2003, the Rotary Club of Marblehead, as part of a celebration of its 80th anniversary, presented the town with another plaque (also written by this author) commemorating Marblehead's wickies (the Light keepers). It was ceremoniously unveiled by the descendants of the wickie families, along with a full roll call of the keepers.

A September 2013 thunderstorm brings dramatic cloud formations bending over Marblehead Light.

Chapter Ten

Postscript

With modern computer technology and the ease of GPS now serving New England ocean navigation, the many lighthouses in our region face an uncertain future, their devoted keepers already a distant memory. Some of the regional lighthouses have been purchased by private owners, renovated, and turned into museums, parks, yacht clubs, or bed-and-breakfast destinations. Many have been decommissioned and torn down; the weather has taken care of the destruction of others.

Today, Marblehead Light continues to operate through two licenses (renewed every six years), one of which gives the town the first right of ownership refusal should the Light be declared surplus by the U. S. Coast Guard. The other license permits the use of the Light tower for a wireless antenna system connecting the Franklin Street Firehouse and the harbormaster to the town's wireless network. We don't know what the future holds for the eventual disposition of the Light.

What we *do* know is that the Light remains brightly lit on the Neck, even if no longer essential to ocean navigation. And while it doesn't resemble the traditional New England brick or stone lighthouse, its tall, spindly structure has its own charm and remains a beloved historic icon for Marblehead townspeople.

With history as much of a love affair for New Englanders as it is, the Light could well continue to be a standing mark of Marblehead's history, a symbol of New England's maritime heritage, and a part of the Northeast's coastal character for years to come. For now, it stands tall on Marblehead Neck at the mouth of the harbor, shining its bright green light proudly out to sea, and offering a welcome to mariners all.

Bibliography

BOOKS

Claflin, James. *Lighthouses and Life Saving Along the Massachusetts Coast*. Charleston, SC: Arcadia Publishing and the History Press, 1998 (and author's conversations with J. Claflin).

Dolin, Eric Jay. *Brilliant Beacons: The History of the American Lighthouse*. New York: Liveright Publishing Corporation, 2016.

Gray, Thomas E. *The Founding of Marblehead*. Baltimore: Gateway Press Inc., 1984.

Holland, F. Ross. *Great American Lighthouses*. Washington D. C.: Preservation Press, 1989.

Marcus, Jon, and Susan Cole Kelly. *Lighthouses of New England*. Stillwater MN: Voyageur Press, 2001.

Samuel Roads. *History and Traditions of Marblehead*. Marblehead MA: N. Allen Lindsey & Co., 1897.

Searle, Richard Whiting. *Marblehead Great Neck*. Salem MA: 1937.

Snow, Edward Rowe; updated by Jeremy D'Entremont. *The Lighthouses of New England*. Beverly MA: Commonwealth Editions, 2005 (originally published 1945; 1973).

WEBSITES

American Lighthouse Foundation, www.lighthousefoundation.org, accessed January 2017

Keepers of the Light: Lighthouse Preservation Society, www.lighthousepreservation.org, accessed January 2017

Lighthouse Digest Magazine, www.lighthousedigest.com, accessed January 2017

Marblehead Musings by Marge Armstrong, www.marbleheadmusings.wordpress.com/category/martin-family, accessed February 2017

National Park Service: *Maritime History of Massachusetts*, www.nps.gov/nr/travel/maritime/mbl.htm, accessed February 2017

New England Lighthouses: A Virtual Guide, by Jeremy D'Entremont, www.newenglandlighthouses.net, accessed January and February 2017

Seeing the Light, Lighthouses of the Western Great Lakes, by Terry Pepper, www.terrypepper.com/lights, accessed January 2017

Acknowledgments

Articles in the *Marblehead Messenger*; *Marblehead Ledger*; *Marblehead Reporter*; *Salem News*; *Lynn Item*; *Lighthouse Digest*, Wells, Maine; the Massachusetts Historical Commission, Boston; and Town of Marblehead Selectmen's minutes and other town records.

Marblehead Museum (formerly the Marblehead Historical Society) for research assistance.

Marblehead Light Tower Inspection reports, provided by the Department of Transportation, U. S. Coast Guard, Civil Engineering Unit, Real Property Branch, Warwick, RI. (The author is grateful to this unit for providing copies of Marblehead Light Advertisement of Bids 1895; Marblehead Light Tower Inspections from 1910, 1927, and 1931; topography layouts; drawings of the new tower; and Light tower licenses.)

The uniform members of the U. S. Coast Guard for their participation in the 2002 Rededication of the Light, with special gratitude to Rear Admiral Vivien Crea and Captain Daniel May.

Marblehead Light tower's door mantel includes a rounded moulding featuring a gold star.

PERSONAL CONVERSATIONS, for which the author is indebted to:

Janet Drayton, granddaughter of Light keeper Henry Drayton

Barbara Drayton Kiernan, great-granddaughter of Henry Drayton and Dana Kiernan

The late Barbara Rogers Mace, born in the Light in 1935, and her husband Alan Mace

Martha Bailey Woodfin, great-great granddaughter of Light keeper James S. Bailey

Karin Martin, descendant of Light keeper Jane Clemmons Martin

Marge Gallo Armstrong, descendant of Jane Clemmons Martin

Harry Wilkinson, the late Marblehead historian and writer

Marblehead Light Historical Timeline

1831: Marblehead Town Meeting approves a proposal to erect a lighthouse.

1833: Marblehead residents approve the lighthouse location on Point of Neck (Marblehead Neck) and the purchase of 3.97 acres for $375 for its location.

1834: Congress appropriates $4,500 for the construction of a modest, 23-foot-tall white stone lighthouse and outbuildings, including a keeper's dwelling and connecting walkway, and construction commences.

1835: Marblehead's first lighthouse is illuminated.

1878: The keeper's dwelling is rebuilt, and improvements to outbuildings continue.

1880s: Complaints are lodged by fishermen and sea captains about the ineffectiveness of the Light, due to its short stature relative to the increasing density and size of nearby residential buildings.

1883: A temporary 100-foot mast with lantern is erected adjacent to the Light, in response to mariners' complaints. The lantern is hoisted nightly.

1893: The U. S. Lighthouse Board approves a new 100-foot lighthouse on the Neck.

1894: The original Light is condemned by the federal government and slated for demolition to make way for the new tower.

1895: The firm of Chamblin, Delaney & Scott (Richmond, VA) is chosen to build the new Light and a foundation is poured in December for a new openwork light tower.

1896: The new Light tower is first illuminated with a steady white light, and the old 100-foot ancillary mast is dismantled.

1922: The Light undergoes a change in fuel, from whale oil to electricity. Its color is changed from white to ruby, c. 1922.

1938: The Light color is again changed, this time from ruby to green.

1941: The Light goes dark under U. S. Army occupation during World War II, relit in 1946.

1947: Marblehead voters agree to accept the deed from the federal government conveying ownership to the town of the Light's land for park use. Resident and Light land abutter Chandler Hovey steps up to provide the necessary funds for this conveyance ($5000). Parkland around the Light is named Chandler Hovey Park.

1956: The in-ground footings beneath the Light's eight pilings are replaced by W. C. Peach Contractors.

1959: The Light keeper's house is demolished and a new brick building is constructed for public restrooms at Chandler Hovey Park.

1960: Marblehead Light is fully automated.

1987: The Light is added to the National Register of Historic Places.

1992: The Light is sandblasted and repainted its traditional metallic brown.

1996: The Light is first decorated with colored lights. The lighting tradition continues to this day, during the Christmas season and the Fourth of July, courtesy of the Rotary Club of Marblehead.

2002: The Light is formally rededicated during a ceremony at Chandler Hovey Park.

2003: The Rotary Club of Marblehead presents the town with a plaque commemorating the Light's keepers (wickies), unveiled by descendants of the wickie families.

2010: The Marblehead Harbormaster's office assumes management of the Light tower (the structure only).

On the door of the Marblehead Light tower is a plaque (INSET) with dates and information about the Light. It mentions Ezekial Darling as the Light's first keeper but erroneously lists him as a gunner on the USS *Constellation*, not the USS *Constitution*.

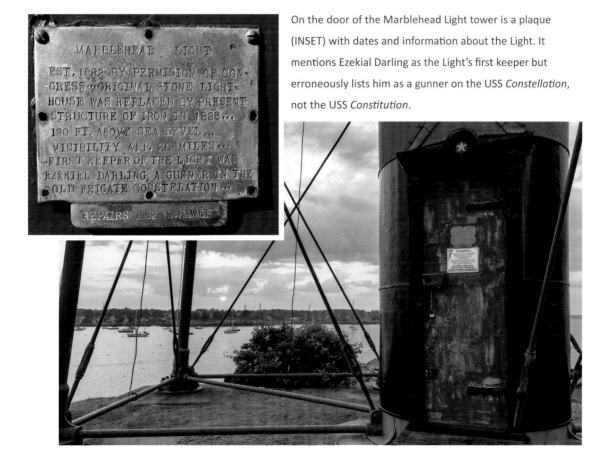

Index

Page numbers in **bold** refer to illustrations

TOP: The lens room is at the very top of Marblehead Light. The lens, shown here still shining just after dawn, is illuminated at dusk and extinguished at sunrise via an electronic timer.

MIDDLE: The Light's center column features an internal spiral stairway with 127 steps up to the balcony level (at right). From there, a small interior ladder leads up to the lens room through a ceiling trap door.

BOTTOM: At the balcony level, an exterior metal ladder allows outside access to the lens room.

Illustration Credits

(MHC: Town of Marblehead Historical Commission)

Outside cover:	Courtesy of Eyal Oren, Wednesdays in Marblehead, © 2017
Back cover:	Inset: Courtesy of MHC
Page 1:	Courtesy of Marblehead Museum
Pages 3, 5:	Both courtesy of MHC
Page 6:	Courtesy of David Cleaveland, Maine Imaging, www.maineimaging.com
Page 8:	Both courtesy of MHC
Page 9:	Courtesy of Renee Conly
Page 10:	Both courtesy of Amy Drinker
Pages 12–13, 14:	Both courtesy of MHC
Pages 16–17:	Courtesy of Marblehead Museum
Pages 18, 19:	All courtesy of MHC
Page 20:	Courtesy of Library of Congress
Page 21:	Courtesy of MHC
Pages 22–23:	Courtesy of Marblehead Museum
Page 24:	Left: Illustration from *Les Merveilles de la Science* [1867–1869] by Louis Figuier
	Right: Courtesy of United States Lighthouse Society
Page 25:	Top: Courtesy of MHC
	Bottom: Courtesy of Marblehead Museum
Page 26:	Top: Courtesy of Encyclopedia Britannica
	Bottom left: Courtesy of www.terry pepper.com/lights/closeups/illumination/
	Bottom right: Courtesy of United States Lighthouse Society
Page 27:	Top: Courtesy of Marblehead Museum
	Bottom: Courtesy of MHC
Page 28:	Top: Courtesy of Kraig Anderson, www.LighthouseFriends.com
Pages 28–29:	Bottom: Courtesy of MHC
Page 30:	Both courtesy of Bill Conly
Page 31:	Top: Courtesy of MHC
	Bottom: Courtesy of Marblehead Museum
Pages 32, 33, 34–35:	All courtesy of MHC
Page 36:	Courtesy of Janet Drayton
Page 37:	Both courtesy of MHC
Page 38:	Both courtesy of National Archives, www.LighthouseFriends.com
Pages 40, 41:	Both courtesy of Bill Conly
Page 42:	Inset: Courtesy of MHC
Pages 42–43:	Large image: Courtesy of National Archives, www.LighthouseFriends.com
Page 44:	All courtesy of MHC
Page 45:	Courtesy of Marblehead Museum

Page 46:	Top: Courtesy of Bill Conly
	Bottom: Courtesy of Marblehead Museum
Page 47:	Courtesy of Amy Drinker
Page 48:	Top: Courtesy of Dick Carlson
	Bottom: Courtesy of MHC
Page 49:	Top: Courtesy of MHC
	Middle: Courtesy of Janet Drayton
	Bottom: Courtesy of Amy Drinker
Page 50:	Courtesy of MHC
Page 51:	Top (both): Courtesy of MHC
	Bottom: Courtesy of Janet Drayton
Page 52:	Courtesy of Janet Drayton
Page 53:	Top: Courtesy of Barbara Rogers Mace, Lighthouse Digest
	Bottom inset: Courtesy of MHC
	Large image: Courtesy of Bill Conly
Page 54:	Courtesy of MHC
Page 55:	Courtesy of Amy Drinker
Pages 56–57:	Courtesy of Marblehead Museum
Page 58:	Courtesy of Bill Conly
Page 59:	Courtesy of Fred Sullivan
Pages 60–61:	Courtesy of Gene Arnould, Arnould Gallery
Page 62:	Both courtesy of MHC
Page 63:	Top: Courtesy of MHC
	Bottom: Courtesy of United States Lighthouse Society
Pages 64–65:	Courtesy of Eyal Oren, Wednesdays in Marblehead, © 2017
Page 66:	Top (both): Courtesy of Bill Conly
	Bottom left: Courtesy of Marty Riskin
	Bottom right: Courtesy of Bill Conly
Page 67:	Top (both): Courtesy of Bill Conly
	Bottom right: Courtesy of Amy Drinker
Pages 68–69:	Courtesy of Eyal Oren, Wednesdays in Marblehead, © 2017
Page 71:	Courtesy of Amy Drinker
Page 73:	Inset: Courtesy of Amy Drinker
	Large image: Courtesy of Eyal Oren, Wednesdays in Marblehead, © 2017
Page 75:	Top: Courtesy of Jack Attridge
	Middle: Courtesy of Amy Drinker
	Bottom: Courtesy of Eyal Oren, Wednesdays in Marblehead, © 2017

Special thanks to Rick Ashley for photographing objects and paintings and for digital editing expertise.